Adva.... .....

Somos Nopales

There's an indelible truth to that old saying, "cultura cura." And evidence of its power radiates from the pages of Eddie Vega's *Somos Nopales*. At the heart of this collection is the struggle to overcome the sense of dislocation when one is "ni de aquí ni de allá," and the perseverance it takes to find home—not in any particular house or even country—but in the words, people, and even foods that thrive in the borderlands, where everything comes together, though not always harmoniously. Vega's candid poems pay tribute to the place where all belong—Nepantla. And if this place is unknown to you, after reading Vega's evocative book, it will become the place you'll want to be.

—Rigoberto González, author of *The Book of Ruin*

Poetry that leaps off the page, like a bolt of electricity from a Tesla coil, pero also brown and HILARIOUS and poignant and brilliant.

—Gustavo Arellano, columnist for the *Los Angeles Times* and author of *¡Ask a Mexican!*

"Because I am a poet,/I picked up my tools,/I went to work today," Eddie Vega says and then demonstrates the heart-driven labor of speaking his truths of roots, family, identity, and life. Writing about what he's made of, Vega lists "My kids' laughter, all of it/un poquito de heartache/demasiado heartbreak/un splashito of hope" because that's what it takes to keep going, to keep dreaming, to keep fighting, to reroot and rise again in the face of struggle. These poems are the sharp spine of the nopal, but also the tender life-giving nourishment of its flesh. Eddie Vega is nepantlero, poeta, teacher, voz, y todo corazón.

—**ire'ne lara silva**, 2023 Texas State Poet Laureate

Somos Nopales

FLOWERSONG
PRESS

poetry by

Eddie Vega

FLOWERSONG
PRESS

For Adrienne,

you helped me reach my next level

Prologue

I was in the middle of a delicious nap – the kind of nap where there's no dreaming, just placid darkness and you end up with a pillow with sweat from your head and drool from your mouth. It's the kind of nap that, upon waking, leaves you in an existential conundrum. You don't know what day it is, what time it is, what your name is, what your purpose is, what the sound from that device on your nightstand really signifies, but you answer the phone anyway. This is the nap I was in when my father called about his confusion with the census. I was annoyed, confused, perturbed, disturbed, what my mother refers to as, a bear.

"Hello"

"Hey! ¿Como estas? ¿Que andas haciendo?"

"Well, I was napping, but then the phone rang."

"Yeah, who was it?"

It was hard to make out polite words so I didn't answer that question.

"Anyway, what are we?"

"What are we? You're my father."

"No, that's not what I mean."

"We're blood relatives."

"No. Listen. I'm filling out the census form. Have you done yours yet?"

"No, I was going to, but I got sleepy and decided to take a nap."

"It says: 'What is Person 1's race? Mark X,' osea tiene una X in the box, 'mark one or more boxes AND,' *and* está in capital letters, 'print origins. White. Print, for example, German, Irish, English, Italian, Lebanese, Egyptian, etc.'"

"I don't think that's us."

"'Black or African American. Print, for example, African American, Jamaican, Haitian, Nigerian, Ethiopian, Somali, etc.'"

I sighed. He kept going.

"'American Indian or Alaska Native. Print name of enrolled or principal tribe' or tribes, 'for example, Navajo Nation, Blackfeet Tribe, Mayan, Aztec,' Hay Mayans y Aztecs aquí? 'Native Village of Barrow Inupiat Traditional Government, Nome Eskimo Community, etc.'"

"Dad"

"Y luego tiene, 'Chinese, Filipino, Asian Indian, Other Asian,'"

"Dad!"

"'Vietnamese, Korean, Japanese, Native Hawaiian, Samoan, Chamorro?' Chamorro is a race?"

"DAD!"

"'Other Pacific Islander.' What do you think?"

"Did you just read the whole section to me?"

"Well how else are you going to know what I'm talking about?"

"Ugh. I guess."

"So what do I put?"

"Pos no se. There's got be somewhere that we fit."

"Pos I don't see us anywhere."

"I don't know. I just don't know!"

"Porque te enojas? You should probably take a nap. You sound cranky."

I wonder if this explains my poetry – a cranky response to having been suddenly awakened. So many times, I've sat and written something after an event or a comment that pissed me off.

My father's lessons sometimes take decades for me to understand. This one only took two weeks. I wrote the first poem in this collection as a response to feeling bewildered by the census form.

The form isn't the first time I've felt this way – like I don't fit, don't belong, don't count. I'm the son of an immigrant, grandson of a woman born in Texas who hardly spoke English. My maternal grandmother didn't need to speak the language, as she lived in a pocket of America where it wasn't necessary. In order for me to belong in this country I was formally educated away from the culture of my family. Spanish was my first language, but I've been losing it ever since I started learning English from Mrs. Aguilera, my kindergarten teacher at Woodrow Wilson Elementary in McAllen, Texas.

"No soy ni de aqui, ni de alla." I'm not from here nor from over there. It's the plea of every Mexican-American. Our Mexican cousins ridicule us because we can't roll our Rs and have trouble finding words to describe what we're trying to say, while our American friends are quick to point out that we have an accent when we talk.

I've been trying all my life to fit in in a country that still sees me as other. I spent my tween and teen years trying to assimilate, rejecting salsa on my food, conjunto music on the radio, and Spanish on my tongue. I've spent the next few decades trying to recover the Mexican parts of me, going so far as to spend my first year after college in Veracruz.

Coming to terms, however, with the fact that *no soy ni de aqui ni de alla*, I've spent the bulk of my thirties and now forties accepting myself as a Chicano of the Tejano variety. I embrace flour tortillas, enchiladas made of red tortillas and topped with yellow cheese, and the facility of mixing my English con español cuando me de la gana.

I've come to terms with being a *Nepantlero* – inhabiting a region that is geographically, metaphysically, cosmically, in-between. Gloria Anzaldua grew up in the next town over from mine, but her works were never taught to us. Today, she gives language to my understandings.

> "Like all people, we perceive the version of reality that our
> · culture communicates. Like others having or living in more
> than one culture, we get multiple, often opposing messages.
> The coming together of two self-consistent but habitually

incomparable frames of reference causes un choque, a cultural collision." (from *Borderlands/La Frontera: The New Mestiza*)

Maybe this is why some have described me as chocante. Though truthfully I'm not sure if I'm still in the collision or living its consequences.

I hear poets give a five-minute introduction to a two-minute piece and often scream, "just read the damn poem!" (In my head, of course.) But I know the feeling of wanting to explain more of what goes into each line, why some words mean more than what is heard, and where each idea came from.

My life is in the footnotes of my poetry.

The census tried to reduce me to a checkbox. This book is my answers to the questions it could not ask: I'm Chicano, Tejano, Hijo del Quinto Sol, Chocante, American, Mexican, immigrant, Mexican-American, Nepantlero, first-gen, hypertensive, and in debt.

table of contents

IV | Heroes

Somos
Nopales

I

Spirit of
the Nepantlero

Counting

It's been two weeks since my father called
Two weeks since his questions
Two weeks since his confusion
Two weeks since his Hispanic panic

It's been two weeks since my father
          filled out his census form
Two weeks since I told him there must be a category
Two weeks since I told him there must be a place
Two weeks since I told him there must be a box where we fit in

Today I'm filling out my census form
using the eyes my father gave me
looking for a place where we fit in
seeing how two weeks ago
he was right to feel bewildered

What am I?

Not white
No option for Mexican
Hispanic doesn't count

When I wanted to know what color I was
I went to Lowe's, looked at paint swatches
Benjamin Moore calls my skin *San Carlos Tan*

Black and White are the only two options here
I wonder what the government bureaucrat will say
when I write in, "San Carlos Tan"

I don't want to get bogged down in definitions –
race, ethnicity, nationality, but
I'm participating in a national headcount
being made to feel like I don't count at all

Like my mother doesn't count
Like my abuelita doesn't count
Like my gente has never counted

When Julian Castro dropped out of the presidential race
he stated:
   "It simply isn't our time,
   ganaremos un día,
   someday, we'll win…"

I guess people didn't think he counted either
and what does that say about America,
that a Stanford and Harvard-educated man
who speaks better English than he does Spanish,
doesn't count?

When will it be our time?
When will we count?

People with my last name,
my earth-toned skin, two-tongued voice
have lived on this land for five centuries

When will it be our time?

We picked the crops
shipped them in trucks we built
brought the food to your table

When will we count?

We taught your kids
used the lesson plans you gave us
erased our own stories from history

When will it be our time?
When will we count?

We fought in the wars
bled the same color blood
my primo, Benito Antonio Ramirez died
an American flag on his shoulder,
the halls of Montezuma in his heart,
tell me that doesn't count for something

Maybe someday we'll win
today, I just want to survive,
not feel defeated by checkboxes on an online form

I'm picking "other"
that's the most accurate description
of how I've felt in this country

I can count on all the hands of my family
how many times I've been made to feel
like I don't belong

I'm writing in "Chicano"
because this nation was Aztlán
before it was America

And this native-born, San Carlos Tan, Texan
doesn't need some form to define him

I know who I am
It's my time
I count

So Stereotypical

Q. Why do Mexicans eat tamales at Christmas?
A. So at least they'll have something to unwrap

This might be as true as everything else they say about us

My parents, typical Mexicans, brought drugs into the country –
        the pills for my mom's high blood pressure,
        the antibiotics for our ear infections
        Vick's Vapor Rub for everything else

My mother, typical Mexican, got married while she was pregnant –
        she'd already been married to my dad,
        but that wedding was on the other side of the border
        this was the one that really counted
        the one that allowed my father to stay in this country

My father, typical Mexican, came here with nothing –
        except an education and some teaching credentials
        they were honored about as much as a gringo honors
        any agreement

My familia, typical Mexicans, we went on food stamps, but my
father couldn't handle that, so like a typical Mexican, he left us –
        every morning to work long hours and little pay

My father, typical Mexican, stole his job from an American
        or was it another Mexican?
        he took a job that was there
        how can you steal that which hadn't belonged to
        anyone before?

My abuelita, typical Mexican, made the tamales
        wrapped them in corn husks
        wrapped them in foil
        so other Mexicans could unwrap them

Tamales aren't all we have to wrap and unwrap:
        we also wrap a slice of white bread around a weenie,
        call it a hotdog
        wrap a tortilla around yesterday's beans, call it breakfast
        wrap ourselves in San Marcos blankets with pics of
        white-tail deer on them, call it surviving Winter

Meanwhile, Texas wraps caution tape around our history
        forgets the Rangers that wrapped nooses around necks
        continues to wrap false accusations around immigrant
        reputations

Really, we
        wrap ourselves around the employment line
        wrap cords around produce sacks to feed America
        wrap ourselves around a timeclock, call it construction
        of our American dream

Then go home,
        wrap our arms around our familia
        wrap our familia around our faith
        wrap our faith around our hope of a better mañana

Have a party where
        everyone is invited
        everyone is happy
        everyone is drunk   on life
                everyone got there   in the same car
        because we are typical   Mexicans!

Somos Nopales

When I think of a plant, I don't think of a cactus
its form irregular,
no stem, broad leaves,
or leaves that are limbs and
spikes that are leaves,
the oldest with a bark,
but can we really call them trees?
fruit that might look like a pear but sweeter,
adorned with impossible flowers

Cactus pokes out from under rocks,
straddles a fence line
sprouts up next to old brick walls
surrounded by asphalt and concrete

Yet, it was on the cactus that the eagle
was found eating the serpent
on the plant that thrives in arid climates,
whose paddles will cause you pain
on the plant that can be cut,
discarded on the driest of ground,
only to reroot itself and rise again,
refuses to give up or go away,
refuses to die
el nopal is the toughest, most resilient plant on earth

And what does it say about us that we eat nopales?
that we cut the spikes off like they never mattered,
that we wash and rinse and boil

and rinse and drain and sauté,
that we eat the ugliest shrub del monte
the plant rejected, found amid stones,
has become the cornerstone of our Lenten plate,
the Lazarus of our garden

You say ouch,
        we say, y que
you say eeooo, we say,
        dame mas
you say cactus,
        we sing, *nopalitos… se venden nopalitos*
        nopalitos se venden, nopalitos se dan,
        para la sena, para el desayuno, con huevo y tortilla
        nopalitos se venden nopalitos se dan

And someone had to cut the spikes off
then wash it then boil it then wash it again
and someone had to figure that out
so stop saying that we're lazy

And raza, stop being lazy –
we can wash and boil and wash those politicos all we want
but they won't get any more palatable
cast the ballot that casts them out

Somos nopales, we are cactus
let's prosper where we plant ourselves
be a prickly pain to the system
that thinks it can just handle us
be the toughest most resilient transplant on earth
make roots along walls, rise among stones,
flourish in wastelands
they may look away when they see us,
but we cannot be avoided

they succeed only in giving us an unquenching desire
to grow and grow and grow and grow and
grow and grow and grow and grow and grow

they tried to bury us,
they didn't know that we were nopales

nopales nopales nopales
somos nopales!
refuse to die!

Nepantlero

I

To be Mexican-American in a border town means
the river is a fine line that you have to walk across
though sometimes the gait required is a cumbia beat

It means hiding who you are at home
from who you are at school
knowing who you are at school
won't be easily understood at home

It means drowning out the sounds of Roberto Pulido
to fit in with the sounds of Depeche Mode
hiding Fito Olivares from your friends
hiding Public Enemy from your parents

It means dealing with cousins that are still on the other side
en el otro lado
who don't think you're Mexican enough
they think it's just your Spanish that's broken
not your heart,
or your abuelita's, the first time she realized
you couldn't roll an R

It means you can't roll with your white friends –
they live on the nice side of town
it means you hope you don't get rolled in
        by your brown friends –
they live down the street from you

It means you have two identities
you live in two worlds separated by lines
that only become evident when you apply for college

II

The white kids had all the nice shoes and the good genes
advantages in school, computers at home
think you have the advantage because you're a minority
that you got into Notre Dame, Chicago, and UT
because of your last name
forgetting you kicked their ass in Calculus and US History

They formed a "gang" – their word
"klan" – probably more accurate
leaned in, called themselves White Trash
gave themselves a symbol, super-imposed a W and T
then imposed themselves on everyone else
had the privilege to go mudding in their big-wheeled trucks
while you walked home
timing streetlights so you wouldn't be stuck at the corner

III

To be Mexican-American means you answer differently depending
on who's asking
when the question is about where you're from
you never start with the name of your hometown
because you don't believe anybody knows
or cares to know
where it is

You refer to leaving as escaping
you didn't want to be one of those that never came back

but here you are
acting bandido when you're really vendido

No eres de aqui ni de alla
No soy de aquí ni de alla

It means you can drown in the river of disappointment
because hope is an anchor that weighs you down

To be Mexican-American in a border town means
no matter how far you go,
there's always a division –
an ever-present river
regardless of whether you can see it

IV

To be Mexican-American is to be in the middle
to be of a border mindset not fully belonging on either side

To be ni de aqui ni de alla
to lose your Spanish, speak english with an accent
not feeling like one is native over the other

It's watching your mouth
while holding both your tongues
feeling blinded
while seeing what others cannot

To be caught between two worlds
to have two names
not sure of which one will get you into what door
wondering if you'll have to break in order to break out

To be caught between your spouse and your family

to have unanticipated arguments
not feeling like you can explain one side to the other
neither side understands the other
neither side wants to understand the other
each side pulling you in their direction
each side thinking they're right

To be Mexican-American is to be careful
navigating between the expectations of
teachers and supervisors
the responsibilities of familia and raza

To realize that some gifts are curses
that some curses are gifts
el cucuy scares you
disappointment haunts you

V

To be Mexican-American is knowing
you can be claimed as white
when it's convenient to everyone except you

It's to be unsure if you're
Chicano
Latino
Hispanic
Coconut
Wetback
Vendido
Cara de Nopal

It's not going to the demonstration.
afraid of who will see you there
then being shunned because no one saw you there

It's working to make positive change in the world
while only having loose change in your pocket

It's working behind the scenes
while actors think you just sit around all day

It's being asked if you think you're too good
while feeling you're never good enough

To be Mexican-American is to be stoic
not being allowed to be angry
because of what they might say
not being allowed to be sad
because they say you have nothing to complain about
not being allowed to be happy
because not everyone made it as far as you
not being allowed to complain
because that's a luxury only gringos can afford

To be Mexican-American is to be called
gringo in Michoacan, Mexican in Michigan
to be Mexican-American is to be neither
or both
never just one

Top Ten Movies You Need to Watch in Order to Truly Understand the Gen X Mex-Am Experience

10. Fools Rush In
"The white people…are melting!"
The cautionary tale every young person needs to see before starting a cross-cultural relationship.

9. a. Desperado
"So, I'm sitting there, and in walks the biggest Mexican I have ever seen…"

9. b. El Mariachi
The one that started it all for Robert Rodriguez

8. My Family/Mi Famila
"That was a political action. I'm a goddamned revolutionary!"
The trajectory of every Mexican-American family from crossing the river to immigrant struggles to doing your best to have your children be successful only to end up with one of them becoming a writer.

7. The Three Amigos
"It's a sweaterrrr!"
"Would you say I have a plethora of piñatas?"
Okay, so the movie is full of campy stereotypes, but it's still hilarious. Sadly, we had so few movies that we had to accept this one, but where would we be without El Guapo? I mean, "in a way, all of us has an El Guapo to face. For some, shyness might be their El Guapo. For others, a lack of education might be their

El Guapo. For us, El Guapo is a big, dangerous man who wants to kill us…"

6. The Sandlot
Benjamin Franklin RODRIGUEZ

5. American Me
"Don't look at me Little Puppet!" :`(

4. Selena
"Anything for Selenas!"
Some might be upset that our beloved Tejana was portrayed by Jenny from the Block, but it's part of struggle, having to "be more Mexican than the Mexicans, more American than the Americans, both at the same time!"

3. Blood In Blood Out
"Vatos Locos forever, ese!"

2. Stand and Deliver
"Plus two, minus two, fill the hole."
"I killed him. He's decomposing in my locker."
As a teacher, Jaime Escalante is the teacher I want to be. As a student I always felt like those kids - always trying to prove how smart I was and that I belonged.

1. La Bamba
"I just wanna see my daughter!"
"Not my first. Or my last"
"That dude's my brother!"
It offers a quote for just about every moment of our lives.
"Who do they want? Elvis?"
La Bamba is the quintessential Chicano movie, a biopic about one of us:
a farmworker, an artist, both shy and charismatic, a boy in love

with a gringita who made it big only to be lost too soon.

"Ri-tchieeeeeee!"
Sleepwalk plays
Fade to brown

P.S. Honorable Mention:
   Like Water for Chocolate (Because it's actually Mexican)
   A Walk in the Clouds (A fantasy film where Mexicans owned
   vineyards)
   Mi Vida Loca (More of millennial flick)
   Born in East LA (We were too young to really get it)
   Coco (because we saw it with our kids)

La Bamba

This poem is just as much for Luis Valdez
as it is for Ritchie Valens
Luis wrote the phrases that have become integral
to our gente's lexicon

Whenever my sister sees a social media post about something good
I've done, she proclaims,
"That dude's my brother!"

When my mom sees we've been treated unfairly,
"They don't know who they're dealing with,
my grandaddy was a full-blooded Yaqui Indian"
Even though he was actually from Guanajuato

When I get rejected for any poetry submission
"Who do they want, Elvis?"

I couldn't have gotten through the pain of
seeing my kids only every other weekend
if I hadn't driven up their mom's house and said
for no one to hear but me,
"I just want to see my daugh-ter"

When I have that really good
taco de barbacoa on a Sunday morning, I say
"Not my first, or my last…"

And when you look over at your special someone, don't you want
to sing:

"You're mine
And we belong together
Yes, we belong together
Fo-or e-tern-uh-teee, e-tern tern-ih-tee-ee-eee""""

But La Bamba is more than just a few lines
the movie starts and ends with the same instrumental song
Sleep Walk by Santo and Johnny
maybe because the whole movie is just that: a sleep walk
a movement through a dream
a meandering through an unknowing reality
it's a story we know is true, but still can't believe

The story of how someone that looks like us, Mexicanos (even
though he's played by a Filipino)
whose brother looks like us (even though he's played by a Puerto Rican)
can escape the farmworker camp
can leave the urban shack
can buy a house for his mother
Who doesn't want to buy a house for their mother?

Ritchie went from walking his girlfriend home to
driving Donna in his convertible
Come on! Let's Go!
let's go as far as we can
let's reach for the stars
the sky is the limit - the sky is the limit –
the sky // was // the limit

Every time I watch, I tell him:
don't win the toss - don't win the toss - don't win the toss
But he does

Then I scream
don't get on the plane - don't get on the plane –

don't get on the plane
But he does

He always wins the toss and gets on the plane
because that's the most Chicano thing to do -
they convince us that we've won
right before we lose everything

But that's ok, Ritchie rose up again, became immortal
that's what we do!
even if it's our own brother that knocks us down,
we get back up

Ritchie Valens taught us how to dare
Los Lobos taught us how to sing
Luis Valdez taught us how to dream

Porque chicanos on screen can be more than farmworkers
more than housekeepers
more than waitresses

We can be // rock stars!
commanding audiences, conquering stages
y no lo tenemos que hacer en ingles
we can sing in Español even if we can't speak it

And Connie, we're with you right there
throwing laundry in the air
not my Ritchie - not my Ritchie - not my Ritchie

He is our Ritchie
He is our hero
He is our dream become reality
inspiring us, informing us, inviting us,
to a life beyond the barrio

And I am proud to stand here on this stage
and tell the story of Ricardo Steven Valenzuela -
That dude's my brother!

RIIIII-TCHIEEEEE

Chicano Typography

I speak of the elusive and the ever increasingly rare breed: The Chicano

Contrary to popular belief this legendary vato did not die out with the 80s. Yes, he is an endangered species, pero if you look closely, you can still find him, in fact, there are lots (muchos or chingos, if you will) of Chicanos – you may have encountered one without even knowing it

First, there is the Closet Chicano – archaically referred to as the coconut (pero that term is pejorative among the raza these day and we no longer use it), the closet Chicano has a degree - from college sometimes even - he works in an office cubicle, wears a tie, laughs at all the jokes about disadvantaged people, lives in the suburbs, pero at home, he watches novellas, stores leftovers in Country Crock containers, and calls his family on the weekends only speaking Spanish – his name is Lorenzo Aguirre, but everyone calls him Larry Uh-Gwire

Second, is the Convenient Chicano – you've got to watch out for this pinche poser – he forgot he was Mexican until he discovered affirmative action – he got the scholarship and the job – he is starting to feel the pressure of being the token at work and making things up every time people ask him about his people:
"Yeah, I eat tuh-mah-lees at least twice a week
I got the recipe from my aww-bway-lee-ta."
He only drinks Dos XX, fully dressed because he saw it in the commercial that way

Next, the Fairweather Chicano – you only spot this guy around
Cinco de Mayo – you thought he'd come around during 16 de
Septiembre pero he forgot about that day and has been planning
his Cinco de Drinko party since February – a clear indicator of him
not being a true Chicano as no self-respecting vato plans a party that
far in advance. N'mbre, no self-respecting vatos plans anything at all

Then there's the But Chicano:
he's a Chicano, but he's a Republican
he's a Chicano, but, "you don't understand," because he was in the
military
he's a Chicano, but he works for the Border Patrol
he's a Chicano, but he voted for Trump
the But Chicano is sometime referred to by his Mexican name –
Culero

Then there's the Expert Chicano – this is the most annoying cabrón
of all – he won't hesitate to explain all things Mexican to you because
HE KNOWS ALL, HE'S SEEN ALL, HE LIVED IN EL PASO
FOR A MONTH – He's the one that avoids the word "Chicano"
and won't have enchiladas in this town because, "they're not
authentic"

There's also the Güero-Chicano – he grew up on the Southside of
San Anto – his neighbors were Mexican and his friends' moms and
abuelitas fed him – he drinks Lone Star, buys tortillas in bulk and
speaks pocho – so what if he's a white guy and his father was from
Ohio? He's more Chicano than the Culero down the block

Oh and then there's the Moreno-Chicano – also known as the
Blacksican – a much darker version of the Güero-Chicano – his
neighbors introduced him to cumbia, he introduced them to Kanye
– he makes better salsa than the Convenient Chicano – you don't
mind that he dates your prima – she doesn't mind either. He drinks
Modelo.

Finally, there's the Chicano Chameleon – this vato is tricky to spot – you think you're working or going to school with a darker-skinned American until you notice: he drives an Impala, he brings tacos for his friends, handing them out without any pomp or circumstance, he jokes with the custodians -- in Spanish, when he sees you he acknowledges you with a head-bob but only if he thinks you're cool, otherwise, it's just "good morning, Matthew, did you see the memo about the new deadline?"

Chicanos – they're out there. Forreal.

They Gave Us a Month

They gave us a month
well not really a month
they pieced together a half here, a half there
which makes sense
since we're half indigenous, half European
not really a whole people

They don't give us a whole month
they give us a piece of September, a piece of October
which really means the 15 days in September
because as soon as October comes
even the toughest vato will care more
about the chichis than his own identity

They gave us a made-up month
instead of a whole month
or a holy month, like December
when we celebrate the birth of our hermano, Jesús
and the visita of his mamá, Guadalupe
her skin not so dark, not so light
because she's a half-sican like us
but they didn't give us December

They gave us a month that doesn't really exist
to make us feel like we do exist
so elementary teachers
can change their bulletin boards, put up pictures
of Roberto Clemente and Cesar Chavez
because they're the only two that did exist

But where's the picture of Henry B. Gonzales?
son of immigrants from Mexico
first Hispanic in the Texas Senate
he stood up and spoke
in the Texas Senate to block segregation,
they carried Henry B off the floor after twenty-two hours

But where's the picture of Jose Gutierrez?
undocumented immigrant from Guatemala
first US casualty in the Iraq War
they carried Jose off the battlefield after twenty-two years

For Henry B's twenty-two hours
For Jose's twenty-two years
they give us thirty days

About 12% of casualties in Iraq were Hispanic
but there are no numbers
from Vietnam
or Korea
or World War II
or World War I
because back then Hispanics didn't count

They gave us thirty days
which is also the minimum penalty for a second DWI
the government will give you more time for being drunk than for
being Latino

They gave us thirty days
which is what you'd get for domestic assault
which should count for all the times
we got beaten down on our own soil

For 94 Latinos killed by police this year
they give us 30 days

For 56 million Latinos in America
they give us 30 days

We've been here more than 300 years
and they give us 30 pinche days

In 1977, Jimmy Santiago Baca wrote the poem,
"So Mexicans are Taking our Jobs"
today, the unemployment rate for Latinos
is higher than the one for all Americans
we must suck at stealing because it's forty years later
and we haven't stolen all the jobs!

But if we did steal one, I bet they'd give us 30 days
at minimum wage
before shutting the factory and moving it to Mexico
because that's irony

So sabes que ese?!
I'm going to be your stereotype
I'm going to steal the other 335
I'm a Chicano all year long!

Please, America

I come from a proud, yet humble people

My father worked for the city
a toll collector at the international bridge
every Tuesday we'd walk to city hall,
wait with his co-workers
for his boss, Charles –
the white guy with the paychecks

The time was supposed to be 9am, but
if Charles wanted to walk in at noon, he could
not one man complained about waiting for three hours –
better to stand in line than to be considered out of line

Our fathers and their fathers and their fathers
always had to work for someone else
to make a request they'd take their hats off,
hold onto the brim, look at the ground, ask the boss:

Please señor, if you could be so kind pay me a little more,
my wife is pregnant
Please señor, if it's possible, I need some time to take
my child to the doctor
Please señor, it's Christmas…

We sat in the back of the classroom not asking questions
our names weren't found in the American History books
Mexicans didn't exist until America fought a war with them

Our parents taught us about revolutionaries
to inspire us taught us about heroes that looked like us,
knowing revolutions and heroes were of the past
maybe the future
disallowed in the present

They taught us about Los Niños Heroes,
the Boy-Heroes that fought invading Americans
rather than hand over Chapultepec
Juan Escutia, a 15-year-old boy,
wrapped himself in a Mexican flag
so the Americans wouldn't capture it
he flung himself over the wall of the castle to his death

Today, children are wrapped in Mylar blankets
captured by Americans,
separated from parents escaping death

Javier Amir Rodriguez, a 15-year old boy
wrapped himself in the Mexican flag made of his own skin
killed by an invading American in an American city

Maybe the border patrol checkpoint
should've faced the other way
keeping out the real threat – white men in their twenties fueled by
hateful ideologies

Every parent that died on their feet
became an unwilling revolutionary,
a necessary hero as they shielded their children from hate

and I heard:
they tried to bury us, they didn't know we were seeds

We don't need more seeds

our sprouts should be jumping ropes
instead of ducking for cover
we need more children on the playground
than in the burial ground

We don't need martyrs or marchers
We need mothers and fathers

We need more people to just live their lives
shopping for crayons instead of coffins
annoyed at another back-to-school night
instead of frustrated over another funeral

America, we've tried everything else
is it time to go back to our campesino ways?
hold our hat brims as we talk to the white man
stare at the blood-stained floors, pleading:

Please America, we don't ask for much
Please America, if you could be so kind
Please America, keep our kids out of cages
Please America, stop killing us

Cómo Hacer Flirt Con Alguien
after Ebony Stewart

Your smile makes me
crumble like queso fresco
melt like queso Oaxaca
refreshes me like a cold limonada
lifts my spirits like the coldest raspa on the hottest day

It's like fresh pan dulce
        warm and sweet
like green salsa
        warm and making me sweat
like tequila
        warm and making me dizzy

Can we be dizzy together?
No, pos ni modo…

Pero
your eyes are like conchas
        big and bright
I see a barrio rainbow of yellow and pink,
        off-white and brown
11am-sunshine and summertime sunsets in them

When I saw you look at me
it was like I was hit with a chancla across my cheek
        not the one on my face

My heart dances the washing machine
at the melody of your
       Hello
You make feel like all the happy Selena songs
You're my Techno Cumbia
I'm el Chico del Apartamento Cinco Doce

You're a chicharrón con huevo taco from Taqueria
       Datapoint on a flour tortilla so light and fluffy
       it wants to float away
You're a quesadilla de asada from the taco truck on
       St. Mary's St. no one knows is called Regio

With you I'm no longer afraid of el cucuy
or la llorona
or la migra

We endured Trump together
and this quarantine
like a pair of teens hiding from all the authorities

You make me feel invincible
I could go to the Northeast side of town, go from I-10 to 410 and
not end up on 35
b'cuz I always mess that up
but with you I can do anything!

I want to sing like a cenzontle in Spring
be a colibri to your flower-petal lips

I want to know if they taste like chocolate
or cafe con leche
or mole
or a Mexican Coke

or home

What I'm really trying to ask is:
Can we be a pareja or at least share some nachos
        or something?

No?

Pos, ni modo...

Whom would you like to speak with?

My 3rd Grade teacher changed my name
No lawyers were involved
No forms were filled out
No money was exchanged

My 3rd Grade teacher caused me problems at home
My dad still calls me Eduardo
Said he'd call me what he named me
My mom calls me Eddie
Says she just doesn't care as long as they're nice to me when they call

My 3rd Grade teacher wrote me into the general Chicano narrative
Maria became Mary
Ezekiel became Zeke
Consuelo became Connie
Esteban became Steve
Margarita became Margaret
Santiago became Jimmy
Eduardo became Eddie

My 3rd Grade teacher gave me a new identity
Eddie at school
Eduardo at home

Eddie
at school, in the classroom
where I existed in an Anglicized world
of theory and objectivity
systematic theology

romantic poetry
Gin Blossoms and Red Hot Chili Peppers

Eduardo
at home, in the barrio
where I existed in a Hispanicized world
of magical realism and conscientization
teología de liberación
Romanceros Gitanos
boleros tejanos
David Lee Garza y Los Musicales

My 3rd Grade teacher set me on a course of confusion
Some people call me Ed
                    I think of the horse (of course)
Some call me Edward
                    I think they must hate me
Janie at the taqueria calls me Eric
            it's what she heard when I said Eddie after ordering in
Spanish
I was first published as Jerry Vega
                    the editor must've thought I was Puerto Rican
The maintenance guy at school calls me Jesse
                    I corrected him at first, but it's been two years
            it feels awkward to fix it now
Most students call me Vega
                    as if it's a first name
Some students call me Vegs
                    they think it's cool that way
Court papers call me EDUARDO REY VEGA
                    I wonder why they're always mad
At a slam I'm Eddie V.

In Mexico they called me gringo
Nobody calls me Lalo

When the bill collector asks for Eedordoo Veega
I say, in all honesty,
"There's no one here by that name."

Recipe for Eddie

Ingredients:

1 pint, Mama's eyes
1 gallon, Dad's wit
2 pints, cachetón-ness
12 cups of torture from my sister
a pinch of salt
Too many First Fridays (yet never enough)
1 order of quesadillas from Tacos Regio
    at midnight on St. Mary's Street
1 breakfast taco special (country con huevo)
    from Taqueria Datapoint
a little more salt
1 dozen of Abuelia Tocha's tamales,
    folded with some of her coarse-ground language
Abuelita Ofelia's móle and a dash of her blunt honesty
My kids' laughter, all of it
un poquito de heartache
demasiado heartbreak
un splashito of hope
more or less equal parts: Amado Nervo, Trinidad Sanchez,
Carmen Tafolla, Jesse Cardona, Stevie Ray Vaughn, Selena,
Freddy Fender, Pedro Infante, Los Lobos, The Texas Tornados,
George Strait, and Norah Jones
1 acordión (note: do not substitute an accordion as it changes
the consistency)
1 rose, beautiful, uprooted in Raleigh,
    replanted in San Antonio
OK, whatever, some more salt

Mix familiar ingredients and ⅓ of salt in an RGV-sized bowl. Place under overcast skies. Sprinkle mixture into sunny days in the high 90s. Mix well while listening to chicharras at mid-morning. Simmer while listening to All Things Considered. Add rose (or maybe let the rose add you).

Throw remaining salt over left shoulder

Add sighs, to taste

Keep simmering, you're only 47

I Demand a Recall

Those Reebok Pumps I had back in 1991
didn't do a thing for my basketball skills.

I used to think it was because the left one
would lose air after about eight steps,

but now I'm wondering if the whole concept
was flawed, so I was thinking maybe I'd start

a class action lawsuit against them, as I'm sure
I'm not the only one they didn't work for, but

then I thought about how much I've enjoyed
my career in education and had those shoes

worked like they were supposed to, I'd be
so busy in the NBA that I wouldn't have had time

to hone my classroom skills.
Maybe I'll send Reebok a thank-you card.

Poet at Work

If you're wondering about my day,
I'll tell you
It starts with:

Huevos rancheros, corn tortillas, made by hand
The beans need un poquito de sal
A father and son sit on the same side of the table sharing
        elbows and shoulders
Occasionally the larger head rests on the smaller one,
        saying mijo, I love you

A woman, sharp black eyeliner and cheetah print leggings
        talks to the older woman across from her that wears the
        same eyes and nose, and says
        "Come live in my apartment, Mamá.
        I'll take care of you."

Someone left the newspaper behind, headlines that read:
Body Found on Westside Still Unidentified
Texas Legislature passes Open Carry and Cuts in Education
GOP denies being racist despite surge of Donald Trump
Did you catch the latest episode of Dancing with the Stars?

At Brackenridge Park two trees full of white cranes
        drown out the sounds of children on the playground
        while I stare at a lone cottonwood leaf, rolling down a
        marked trail

Afternoon at the library:
homeless men taking naps at window-side tables
            opened books of architecture and Renaissance
            masters in front of them
at the book cellar, I find copies of Ulysses and Frankenstein

I've thought about my children eleven separate times
how much I miss them and how much I hate divorce
I've thought about my mother's Crohn's, my father's stress
my sister, her husband, my cousins –
            both foreign and domestic
Mrs. Aguilera, who in kindergarten taught me that
'I' is for Iguana in both English and Spanish
a former student that introduced me to his girlfriend
            as his mentor
his classmate, who told me he liked doing the Sunday
            puzzle on Morning Edition,
            two months after he got clean
            18 months before he found a permanent way out
his cousin, who reached out to tell me the news

All day I've breathed in fresh tortillas and stale coffee
cumin and cigarettes,
rose petal rosaries and mountain laurel trees
Tennyson and Yeats
Whitman, Ginsburg, Bukowski,
Gil Scot Heron, Amado Nervo, Pablo Neruda,
Jesse Cardona, Carmen Tafolla,
Freddie Fender, George Strait, Stevie Ray Vaughan,
and Selena

No! I didn't build your new Texas Tundra,
pick the lettuce for your salad
lay new asphalt for your ride home

serve sweet tea to sour tourists
or physically defend your freedom

But I stared in the eyes of those who did
honored to walk among the farm workers and
          factory workers,
servants and soldiers

Their toil is my strength
Their sweat is the ink which flows through my pen
Their grunts, groans, and sighs I translate to be their voice

Because I am a poet,
I picked up my tools,
I went to work today

II

Geography of
the Nepantlero

Catching Ashes

We'd jump as high as we could
pretending we were Drew Pearson or Tony Hill
catching ashes
like passes
from Danny White

Somebody,
maybe it was Coach Soto,
said the ashes were from sugar cane
burning in Reynosa

I imagined tall, brown stalks
being raised in big, square fields
withstanding blazing summers
succumbing to intentional fires

Quien sabe...

All I actually saw
were small, black flakes,
smaller versions of the carbon paper
my mom used on her typewriter
descending from a cloudless sky
moving with a breeze I barely felt

They'd crossed the river without effort,
an international boundary,
bypassing the Border Patrol
without reporting to the INS
with nothing to declare to the Customs officer

Years later,
my cousins stand in lines to get special permissions
seeking refuge from nooses and gunshots
soldiers without uniforms to wear
or battle lines to shoot from
they have nothing to declare
but the fact
that they'd been raised in the wrong fields
withstanding blazing summers
asking only to be given the opportunity
to escape from intentional fires

Home on the Border

It's been too long since I've been home

Too long since I traded mesquite and brushland
for live oak and hill country
So long that I don't know If I'm still allowed to call it:
Home

I grew up in a town with fewer people
than my current zip code
where there are about two degrees of separation –
if people don't know your mom or your dad,
they know your cousin
or your other cousin
or the guy who you thought was your cousin
because he was at all the pacahangas
until you realized that you were only blood-related
to about four people at those gatherings
including your parents and your sister

We were always last in the Valley:
the last ones to get the newest movie
or the hit song on the radio
or that pair of shoes we could see on TV
but not buy at Academy until a month later

The last one to get the news

They used to say that if America was ever attacked
with nuclear weapons,
we'd be the last ones to hear about it

Did you know that the last battle of the Civil War was fought near
Brownsville?
they had to stop the battle in the middle of the bombardment to tell
the troops
that the war had been over a month before?

Even our firsts were lasts
first, in poverty
first, in highest unemployment
first, in the amount of drugs smuggled through our border

First, to get the Border Wall
first, to be separated from our relatives by concrete
because water wasn't enough

Yet, also place of my
first crush
first kiss
first rejection
first bully
first beach
first funeral
first publication
first accolades

The Valley seems like the perfect place to escape from
Some days it seems like the perfect place to escape to

Woodrow Wilson Elementary

Fuimos a la Wilson
My hermanita only had to go to kindergarten
for half of the day
because she knew English already

It was the second half
after The Three Stooges and right when the musiquita to the Perry
Mason would start
(tah-taaaaaahn tah-tah, tah-taaaaaaah tah-tah...)

But I had to go the whole day
because I didn't know English yet
Mrs. Aguilera was my teacher
she had the letters on a soga with animales for each one
A is for Anteater, B is for Bear, C is for Cat, D is for--
Mees, Rolando says I smell like a dog!

We were the Wilson Warriors
Which is why they made us buy red tablets that said:
Big Chief
and pencils that said:
Ticonderoga
so we could all practice our letters

Then they made us sit
Indian style
so we could all practice how to be silent and still
we sang:
One little, two little, three little Indians...

so we could blend in with the rest of the gringitos
who knew all the best racist songs

Mrs. Gutierrez
didn't have to hand me a bible or cut my hair
She whitened my skin by
clipping my tongue so it didn't roll anymore
changed my name from Eduardo to Eddie

I left that school in third grade because
they thought I was smart
so they sent
me to a classroom with white kids

And somewhere before my sister finished her years there
they tore down the school to build a new one in its place
they got rid of every outdated structure
they kept the name and the mascot

Por Vida Lessons

It was at La Lamar
that I learned Chicanidad, Cholo Poetics,
Vato Logic, and Barrio Geography
specifically in P.E.,
the only class not designated G/T

Barrio boundaries weren't on the school board's map
so my schoolmates marked walls and stalls to designate their
territorial geography:
La Alvarez
La Navarro
El Campito

In Cholo Poetics, vocabulary and syntax
were taught experientially
I learned that one does not say, yes
Simón – will suffice
unless you want to address one of your camaradas directly, in which
case,
Simón, ese – is the preferred form

The barrio is a space where natural laws are suspended
written rules go ignored
unwritten rules are carved into the invisible stones
used to wall out the invaders:
> Logic
> Reason
> Science

Huevos are testicles,
but one can both, have testicles and not have huevos
at the same time
it's called the Law of Non-Contra-Que-Dices

Barrio Logic follows this same axiom
like when Nando said I was talking shit about him
I said, no I'm not,
he responded, are you calling me a liar?
      I was confused
      he was sure
that's when I knew I had failed Intro to Vato Logic

Chicanidad said that a big white t-shirt and a pair of jeans
was just as good of a uniform as khakis and a polo

For some, at least
I was not some
I was not that
I was not ese
I was not that guy
I was not ese vato

Maybe the vatos de mi barrio thought I was going somewhere
so I couldn't go with them

Chava was some
Chava was that
Chava was ese
ese vato
ese vato was quiet, but not quieto
ese vato had huevos
answered roll call from Coach Martinez with: Simón
in his cut-off Dickies and white shirt

you can't say he was going nowhere
prison is somewhere

Ese vato inquieto shot a cop at a quince
dicen que he was defending
the barrio boundary lines being ignored
when he and his camaradas turned the civic center
into a por vida lesson

He graduated early, at 17
went from juvi to gen pop

I guess we both made it out of the barrio, or
we're each stuck in our world and not stuck in the barrio, or
the barrio is both a location and a situation –
it's Chicanidad, Cholo Poetics, Vato Logic, Barrio Geography

Simón, ese

El Hey She Bee

The barrio's grocery store is called Hey She Bee
tiene de todo

In the produce section:
naranjas and grapefruit
lemons and limones
onion, tomato, jalapeño, cilantro, and apio
also collard greens and mustard greens
plus exotics like broccoli and asparagus

The carnicería,
has the usual cuts -
seven steaks, fajitas, short ribs, and spare ribs
plus gringo cuts like rump roast and Boston butt
brisket is stored under lock and key
pork and poultry always in stock
barbacoa on Saturday and Sunday only

The deli has ham and bologna
plus the two types of cheese – yellow and white

The panaderia has more than just pan dulce
tambien rye and sourdough, pero in limited quantities
the tortilla aisle also has sliced bread
and buns para los hot dogs

Of course there's an entire aisle con foreign food –
Vienna sausage, pimento cheese,
all the stuff to make the casseroles

En el business center hacen todo:
cashean cheques
sendean money orders
venden lottery tickets
te dan el registration para tu car or truck
una de mis friends even got her divorce there

In the morning, huele a Fabuloso
in the afternoon, elotes
and at night, puro sudor from all the people
that just got off the day shift

El Hey She Bee del barrio is smaller
than the ones in the fancy parts of town
pero tiene de todo

Nogalitos

The Southside street sounds so sweet
reminding me of
pecans

But as I crack these shells, all I get are questions:

Were there pecan trees all along the trail
that flowed south from downtown toward the road to Laredo?

Were they small then?
too young to be nogales?
or just too cute not to -ito them?

Did the first Southsiders lay in hammocks in their shade
cracking nuts and throwing shade
at comadres caminando en la calle?

Where did the arbolitos go?
uprooted by those planting roots along the road?
pushed aside in the name of gente-fication?

What did it sound like
when the cracking stopped
because the company wanted to leave the shellers penniless
by giving them a penny less, per pound?

Emma Tenayuca lead the workers in their walkout
confronting police and paper-shell politicos?
All they wanted was the sweet taste of justice
instead of bitter communistic accusations

Nogalitos,
A.G. Pickard Pecans collects pecans
and aluminum cans
Maria's Cafe serves meatloaf on Thursday
in case you're bored of carne guisada
The underpass is most appreciated at night,
driving with the windows down
the train passing over our heads

All of this I ponder
as Anthony The Poet shows me the taco truck
where I can get cinco de asada for $5.25
knowing that this street is probably the only one that remembers
when the hair on his chinny-chin-chin
was black

Nogalitos
I don't have to dig too far under your smooth surface
to find

sweetness

Brackenridge Park

The grass here is watered with
Shasta Cola, Capri Sun, and Miller Lite
fertilized by egg shells and confetti,
only the confetti is every child smile left to linger in the air
before transforming into gaggles of giggles that
mix with the jabbering of those cranes
who've been chismeando in those trees
since the Payaya first brought their kids
to these river shores

It was here
that I wrote a letter in ink made of tears
on the back of a cottonwood leaf
I sent it on a breeze
I knew no one would ever feel
it's become part of this air
another legend left behindin this park
you might call Brackenridge
we sometimes call:
        Saturday Picnic
        Morning Nature Walk
        Sunday Grilling While the Kids Walk the Stone Blocks Over
        the River

Eventually,
my children will reach that playscape
the mysterious building that we can only speculate about
really it's all legend now
it will always be legend because this park

is older than our great-grandparents
who came here with their parents
maybe it was a bathhouse for early '09ers
or a mule stable for 1929'ers
or probably just cages for the zoo

But to my children it was a castle
and in their legend they defended it
from an invading force of rival seven-year-olds,
brown squirrels, and the fiercest pigeons known
this side of San Pedro Creek

I packed us peanut butter and jelly sandwiches
fruit snacks, granola bars,
fresh strawberries, and juice boxes, so
I could save enough for three tickets on the Eagle
we were all aboard
hearing the conductor's tales of watching bear tails
scurry off into the woods after screaming into the tunnel
then get off the train at Japanese Tea Gardens
count the number of fish and turtles we could spot
before getting back on the train
back toward the zoo
toward the parking lot
toward one more view of this river
before the freeway journey home

And I hope that they remember this legend
how this park always smells like fajitas and felicidades
sounds like squeaky swings and squawking birds
tastes like the pecans we just picked up and cracked open
feels like a breeze that only exists
here

Decomposition

In nature
the carcass decays slowly, over time
each day inviting new creatures
to pick at the remnants of what was once vibrant

> The '02 Ford Escort was abandoned
> at the Church's Chicken at the corner of
> Culebra and San Felipe
> on a Monday afternoon

The first scavengers arrived that night
or maybe Tuesday morning
ate all four wheels

> Wednesday
> the hood was up
> the car was down
> one battery

Thursday
wires and hoses sprang from inside the car
no longer tethers to larger parts needed
for another carcacha in the community

> Friday
> the car woke up without seats
> they now adorn the front porch
> of a house on San Joaquin

Saturday
ants appeared
carried off bits and pieces
wires and fuses
one headlight

                                        Sunday
                            the vultures rested
                                  or were tired
                              or'd had their fill

Monday
a crane appeared
cradled the Escort bones onto a flatbed

                                    It was over
                    or it started over somewhere else

the circle of life in the barrio

Emptied a Whole Clip

I woke up at 5am to the sound of gunshots
outside my window
The 911 operator asked how many
I said it sounded like they emptied the whole clip
because at five in the morning, apparently
I'm gangsta enough to use a phrase like
"emptied a whole clip"

She asked if I'd seen or heard anything
before or after the gunshots
I said, no!
before the gunshots I was asleep
because it was five in the morning
and afterwards, no!
because I'm not stupid
I'm the nosey neighbor that opens the door
to see what's going on when I see
police or ambulance lights I poke through my blinds
but when I hear gunshots
I stay my ass inside and away from the windows

Two days later
as I stopped into the apartment office to pay my rent
I asked about the gunshots
the rental lady said
I don't know, I'm new
this happened two days ago, how new are you?

She said something about
a possible domestic violence situation, then
we're going to have more patrols
I felt sorry for her
she thought more patrols were going to stop
the assholes out there
who think they can fill their empty hearts with full clips

I woke up at 5am to the sound of gunshots
outside my window
I've already dismissed it as
just another Thursday morning in San Anto
I'm starting to sleep better
I think my neighbors moved out last weekend

I hope they're ok

Gente-fication

Haiku:
Gentrification –
Proof that the white flight
was really just a round trip

If people are going to insist on gentrification
of our neighborhoods,
then the only solution is to insist on the gente-fication
of their neighborhoods
because we want to equality
because make San Anto Great Again
because All Houses Matter?

So c'mon y'all, let's gentefy Stone Oak –
put a bus stop on every corner
with an elote stand and a street preacher

Every stoplight on TPC parkway will have to alternate betweenthe
guys from Victory Church
running out to give you their pamphlet
kids selling candy apples and banana bread
people selling bootleg Spurs shirts
and seasonal vendors with:
Valentine's Day flowers, cascarrones, Easter baskets, piñatas, and
giant blankets with the Dallas Cowboys logo or whitetail deer,
on them

This neighborhood needs a pawn shop
because every soccer mom knows

Aderall don't come cheap
and that James Avery charm is so last year

That Japanese-Cajun-Mediterranean fusion food truck
is cute and all
but we need a vendor that actually moves every so often
so bring on the raspa truck playing the worst version of
"Pop Goes the Weasel" on repeat
cruisin' down the street selling cold treats, and
hot Cheetos and cheese, pickles,
Fred Flintstone orange pushup pops, and dime bags

When I get out of Costco,
I want some dude to offer to wash my windshield
for a few bucks

I want to find the place where you can get
your state inspection sticker
regardless of what kind of shape your car is in
right off Redland Rd.

The only cyclists should be paleta-men on their cart-bikes

There should be cops: everywhere!
slowing down to stare at black Lexus SUVs and minivans of every
make and model

Sure, you can find a Brazilian steak house.
but where's the $4.99 enchilada plate?

We don't need urgent care
we need a curandera, a palm-reader
liquor stores, title loans, payday loans,
and tallboys of Lone Star beer,
a Rios Family Salon next to a Fred's Fish Fry

an HEB that has just two types of bread,
one type of tomato, and 23 varieties of Shasta

Because let's be honest,
that neighborhood is missing the characters that give a
neighborhood character

So watch out!
We're going to gente-fy the Northside
one puro San Anto vato at a time

III

Los Nuevos Nepantleros

Monarchs

The monarch butterfly has one of the longest migrations
of any creature on earth
it travels about 3000 miles
from the forests of central Mexico
to the forests of southern Canada

Not one single monarch survives the journey
instead, each generation pushes the next one northward

they're majestic they're grand
they're perfectly Mexican

We are monarch butterflies
We come from native royalty
We catch winds, ignore borders
wear our brown and our black and our gold
as we dance in the rays of Tonatiuh
hijos e hijas del quinto sol

My familia has been coming north for centuries
My abuelito made it as far the border allowed him
My father crossed over
I've out-traveled him,
I'm pushing my children to go as far as their wings
will take them

Mi gente kept moving north – Dallas, Chicago, Detroit –
never making a round trip
each generation left behind tombstones as stepping stones
for the rest to follow

Maybe you call it assimilation, ese
but we had to adapt to survive
we couldn't blend in with our zarapes and sombreros
we traded them in for button-downs and ball caps

But now I'm afraid my kids have lost the taste
for the nectar of our culture
they lose more knowledge
the more time they spend in classrooms
our feet are losing the rhythms of cumbias and huapangos
my own tongue has grown lazy –
Eduardo doesn't have to roll his R now that he's Eddie

It's not like we can camouflage among the concrete
protect ourselves from the ICE-man
that wants to put us in his net
or the gringo that let no one pass for white in El Paso

They say that the reign of these monarchs will be over soon
their old roosts have been replaced by new retail shops
there's literally no place for them to call home
as they move north
soon they'll only exist in captivity – caged butterflies

The Mexica believed each butterfly
was the soul of an ancestor –
if our ancestors can't find places to rest in this country,
what hope is there for us?
how can they visit if they can't find us?
Día de los Muertos without muertos

I woke up every morning in a country
whose president called my father a criminal

My father is royalty – you can't command a monarch
Neh nemiliztli ahcan hueliti – the journey is not over

The monarchs are coming back in bigger numbers
we can't be kept in captivity
our kids cannot stay caged
you can't send us back to the cocoon

We have wings
We will fly
We will adapt
We will call this place home

Our ancestors will know where to find us

Hallucinations

El Son Mixteca has become an immigrant hymn
it starts by acknowledging how far we are
from the floor of our birth

Ay que lejos estoy del suelo
donde he nacido

Ten days ago
Pablo left the dirt floor where he was born
to collapse on the dirty floor
where he would die
shipped as cargo in a refrigerated truck that didn't cool

It became a sweatbox waiting to become a coffin
100 people in over 100-degree heat took turns breathing
through a hole the size of a mother's broken heart

The difference between a dream and a hallucination is
15 degrees of latitude
30 degrees of heat

Crossing the border they found that the American dream
was really an illusion, a side-effect,
the brain's reaction to a lack of oxygen

I wonder what Pablo imagined
sending money back to his mother?
playing with his little sisters?
finally being able to provide something besides worry?

Did you imagine that Pablo
could walk into an employment office,
read the postings, because
in this dream, he can read English,
in this dream, he can read,
fill out all the forms with
        a real address,
        a real social security number, then,
despite the lack of experience or training steal the job,
driving the forklift from Gerald Thompson of Dubuque, Iowa?

Maybe Pablo just imagined
Freedom
Water
Fresh Air   Air   Air   Air

The administration took turns
blaming them for our problems
while immigrants took turns gasping for air

This is what happens when
we say that you can come from nothing,
work hard, and accomplish your goals
but really mean that the *nothing* you come from
is the name of a town in Iowa or Ohio or Connecticut
not a country called Honduras or Guatemala or El Salvador

This is what happens we only use words like
Illegals
Aliens
Criminals, instead of
Humans   Humans   Humans

that look

like my cousins
like my sister
like my children
like you
like me

Pablo headed north
his remains were shipped south

Ten candles were lit at the cathedral for them
Ten flames danced in the darkness
until they ran out of oxygen

The mixteca song says it's better to die of sadness
than to be so far from home
Pablo knew that both these things are true

Prefiero llorar
Prefiero morir
De sentimiento

Choices

I heard the Border Patrol agent
ask the 3-year-old Honduran girl
to choose which parent should stay with her
when the little girl screamed at her father being removed
that same agent asked her why she was crying
when she was the one that had made the choice

They must not teach child development
at the Border Patrol Academy
or human relations
or human decency
or humanity

These Kids

The school bus stop in front of my apartment
looks like America
full of backwards caps, hoodies, and head scarves

The laundromat is on the next block
every trip there is an exercise in diplomacy
we gesture, we smile, we nod
we hope that we're understood when we say
excuse-me, oh I'm sorry, are you using that basket?

We watch while children,
every shade of toothy smile
run between machines as if
navigating between continents
exploring new frontiers
oblivious to barriers
until they hit walls of dryers

Every mother speaks with her eyes
because "The Look"
knows all unspoken languages

The store next to the laundromat
knows all spoken languages
I've seen the Indian store clerk talk Spanish
to the El Salvadoran dude
who was doing his best to speak Vietnamese
to the guy outside
as they share cigarettes and talk about the Spurs

Down the block,
there's a South Asian grocery store
on the backside of a Thai restaurant
next door to a taqueria
where I saw a Japanese med student
introduce her visiting parents to carne guisada
and people of every nation order tacos

Further down the street,
the abandoned parking lot
has been transformed into a soccer field
because soccer knows all unspoken languages
kids use sticks and stones to mark their makeshift goals
without caring about regulation soccer balls
or lines or grass or being told when they're off sides

These kids get along
held together by their broken English
running and kicking and screaming in the same language

These Congolese, Burmese, Afghan,
Eritrean, Ethiopian, Somali kids
Vietnamese, Filipino, Indian, Pakistani, Iraqi kids
El Salvadoran, Guatemalan, Honduran,
Mexican, Serbian, Croatian kids

These American kids

These kids
        aren't diseases or criminals
These kids
        will out do their parents
These kids
        are going to make America great

Finally

Take Them Back!

I'm sitting at my favorite taqueria having just communicated with a server who assumed my language and though it may not have been these exact words in this exact order or combination, but my immigrant father taught me all that was necessary so that I could say: "un burrito jalisco de asada," and he responded with, "y que gusta tomar?"

"Un sweetee," and I could've said "te azucarado" or "te con azucar," but I know that around here "sweetee" is one word and it's not Spanish, or English really, but it's how we communicate in this part of the world where things only make sense in context – let's face it, a burrito Jalisco is about as authentically Mexican as a clean election, but we consume it anyway

Queso is Spanish for cheese but "kay-so" is the magic that ensues when velveeta and rotel come together – Eddie is English short-hand for Eduardo and I am the magic that ensued when my American mother and immigrant father came together and we spoke Spanish and English at home without fear even though the Spanish came here illegally, and so did the English, and the French, and the German, and the Dutch, Italian, Portuguese, Polish, and Austrian

The African came against their will and was forced to work, the Chinese came to work and lost their free will, the Russian came at the invitation of the president, and the president wants to kick out all of the "illegal aliens" and I've never seen anything more alien than orange skin or an administration do so much that was considered illegal

If you're going to take out the undocumented, go ahead, but while you're at it take the tacos and the tequila and there go your margaritas, and take Cinco de Mayo and find some other reason to get drunk, if you can get drunk at all because all your favorite beers and distilled spirits were born somewhere else

Take the pasta and the pizza, the falafel and the French fry, the stroganoff and the spring roll

And take Melania! She wears it on her face as much as she does on her back: she really doesn't care

King Ranch Casserole

My mother took time to prepare chicken
guisado with garlic and onion
while making a sauce with tomatoes and spices
then preparing tortillas, lightly frying them

All these ingredients would then come together –
chicken filled the tortillas
tortillas rolled up
sauce poured over the tortillas
cheese on top of the sauce
foil covered everything
baked in the oven for about twenty minutes
enough time to make a pot of rice

Enchiladas!

But she never took all those same ingredients
mixed them up so that there was a mass of
tortillas, chicken, rice, sauce, cheese, sour cream
in a ceramic dish and served her family a
King Ranch Casserole

So forgive me for getting a little testy about the conversation behind me
in a teacher's lounge on a Saturday
in the middle of a speech tournament
eating this bastardization of Tex-Mex cuisine

When the gringo said,
"oh, I love this, it tastes like home"

to the gringa that made it who responded
"Oh, so you must be a southerner"

I guess home tastes like the King Ranch:
acres and acres of bullshit, cowshit, and horseshit
owned by white men too chickenshit to admit
they stole it from Mexican families

I guess home must taste like the bell peppers
in the casserole
chile dulce, sweet pepper
the kind that replaced the hot peppers in the dish
because the Southerners that lived north of us couldn't handle the
heat

I guess home must taste like assimilation –
taking the flavor from a culture
so that it blends in with the status quo
becomes bland

Maybe being a Southerner means
having the ability to forget
centuries of slavery
decades of Jim Crow

Maybe being a Southern cook means
having the ability to forget
where the recipes came from
who was allowed to sit where
which door one could enter
Paula Deen and her color-full language

Maybe this casserole is the quintessential South Texas dish
it mixes everything together
doesn't believe in individuality

prefers dry, white meat to dark flesh
all the real flavor stripped away
to be more palatable to mouths
incapable of speaking more than one tongue
named for people that stole with privilege instead of guns
lawyers instead of soldiers

Maybe I'm overreacting
Maybe I'm the racist
Maybe it's just a casserole

IV

Heroes

El Paletero

I just saw our local superhero
El Paletero
park his cart-bike at
La Taqueria

He fueled up with
chorizo con huevo
a cup of coffee
and a smile from his server

Now he's gone –
out making his rounds
patrolling the streets
dealing magic out to
La Gente de la Fredericksburg Rd.

Viejito with a Cane

I stood in line, behind
un viejito with a cane
buying pan dulce and
candles of sagrado corazón

A dozen panecillos, six veladoras,
and one timid cashier
wondering
how he's going to prevent Jesus' Sacred Heart
from breaking

Tío Manuel

The Northern Mexican, or Norteño,
is known for having a dry sense of humor

Tío Manuel is one such Norteño
he was trying to console me as my arm was in a cast
       for the third time in my teenage years

Hey Mijo, I had this friend
he broke his arm and for the six months
lo tenía asina, en un esling
but it was ok porque tocaba la guitarra
and he could still work

On weekends, Tio Manuel lived with his wife
at my grandma's house in Mexico
on weekdays, he was building the road to Robstown

One day, he and Tia Lupe came to stay at our house,
and before I knew about immigration laws,
understood that I lived on a border, or
knew the term "anchor baby,"
my cousin was born

They went back to Mexico
Tía Lupe quit her job as a schoolteacher to raise their
       daughter, meanwhile,
Tío Manuel was building the road to Kingsville

They saved up enough to buy land, and
before I knew about colonias,

learned about the concept of infrastructure, or
realized that most neighborhoods in America
had paved streets,
they built a house and had another daughter, meanwhile,
Tío Manuel was building the road to Corpus Christi

I get nervous shaking my Tío Manuel's hands
his great, big, rough palms are really one big callous
developed from years of dealing with bosses demanding a
            faster pace
a South Texas sun that never quits
the ignorance of people who can sit, claiming
the American dream is being stolen
while immigrants stand to make it possible

He was the Mexican labor force that built his own house
installed the doors that welcomed every hungry relative
installed windows from where my cousins
could look out and dream of a world
beyond the walls their father built

He instilled values, invented stories,
insisted that despite the hardships
we take the time to tell jokes about broken-armed guitarists

The only thing broken in that house is his English
he fixed pipes, wires, cabinets, his own status

I feel guilty clasping my Tío Manuel's hands
they got that way from picking up picks and shovels
all I ever pick up are pens and Expo markers,
compared to him I haven't done a thing
to earn my place in the world he put together
all because I had the fortune of being born on this side of
            the river

He built the road to your hunting lease
built the road that takes you to Spring Break on Port A
and when I say he paved the way for his daughters
to go to the University of Texas,
I mean it literally

Somewhere along his journey he also made his own pathway to
citizenship
Mr. Trump, in this particular case, was right
Mexico doesn't *send* their best –
Tío Manuel and Tia Lupe and my father
came of their own accord
and I'll be damned if you say
they're anything but Americans

"You sabe? You sabe English?"

Abuelito Mateo would stop as he passed me on his way into the house. Or out of the house. Or toward his office. La imprenta. He'd type with just his index fingers. Me, a boy sitting in the patio, reading or playing with cars. Or sitting in the rocking chair watching hormiguitas crawl along the wall. He, the stateliest man in Ciudad Mier, Tamaulipas. He'd stop to greet his grandson with a question that needed no answer but received one anyway.

"You sabe? You sabe English?"

Si Abuelito, I sabe English. He'd smile or laugh or both or hop or whisper yo se or walk on by and turn around. Dicen que he worked on Falcon Dam. Dicen que he was the timekeeper No dicen lo que quiere decir, timekeeper. I imagined my grandfather standing in an office overlooking the work on the dam. Near a window, holding a pocket watch, and at just the precise moment say out loud: "5:00 and all is well, 5:00 and all is well."

Only, my abuelito didn't know English.

Even though gringos would always stop and ask him, You sabe? You sabe English? And he would probably smile or laugh or both or say un poquito or be silent so as not to make the gringo nervous as a little boy who didn't know how to react to such questions.

Si abuelito. Yo se English

Abuelita Tocha

We sat at her table
the round one in her kitchen
in the corner
where all the adults sat if we ever had a party there
where the tub of masa sat if tamales were being made

Each of us eating pan dulce
I liked the piedras
she liked the marranitos
I liked orange soda
she liked coffee
I liked hearing her stories
she liked bingo

If it was after six in the evening,
we knew where to find her:
at the old skating rink that turned into a bingo parlor

When she died
each of her bingo buddies
came to her casket
dropped in some markers and a stack of cards
sending her home with enough materials
to keep the game going

Career Choices

In 7th Grade we had a class called "Career Exploration"
we were encouraged to explore different paths in life
find what our place might be in the workforce

We took vocational tests, aptitude tests,
and vocational aptitude tests
given results, told:

"You can make excellent:
auto mechanics
grocers
retail sales clerks
infantry soldiers.
If you try real hard, boys and girls,
maybe someday you can be assistant managers!"

Our field trip was to McDonald's
they showed us how they make them Big Macs so fast
how they build them boxes to put them in
before we left they made sure we knew
how to punch a time clock

When Ms. Afrentosa asked what our parents did
      we hesitated
before saying things like,
"he fixes cars"
"she works at K-Mart"
"he drives a truck"

What Ms. Afrentosa didn't know was that our parents
were actually:
engineers
accountants
psychiatrists

teachers

They crossed the border with knowledge and experience
but had to leave their degrees and credentials behind

My father was a teacher
he exchanged his white collar for a blue one
        to get a green card

The only time I saw him in a classroom
was when he visited as a parent
listening to teachers talk to him
as if he didn't know about pedagogy
he stood in silence despite having so much to say

My father was the most well-educated toll collector
        on the international border
traded desks in rows for cars in columns
turned a podium into a cash register
people paid a dollar instead of attention

Our immigrant parents left opportunities for themselves
to find better ones for their families
they took the jobs Americans didn't want
so their kids could take whatever jobs they wanted

Our immigrant parents started us on a path

to their American dream

My father stopped being a teacher
so that I could be one

Acknowledgements

This book would not have been possible without the love and support of my wife, Adrienne; our kids, Dominique, Julián, Piper, and Jackson; Mateo and Diana Vega; Thiana and Frank Vera.

Edward Vidaurre, Carmen Tafolla, Jacinto Jesus Cardona.

Gustavo Arellano, Rigoberto González, ire'ne lara silva.

FlowerSong Press, The Macondo Writers Workshop, Gemini Ink, The Mouth Dakota Poetry Project.

Toda la gente de South Texas who act as muses, sources of frustration, and fonts of inspiration.

...and readers like you.

Credits

"Somos Nopales" was originally published as "Cactus" in *BlackBerry Peach Poetry Prizes 2023*. National Federation of State Poetry Societies. 2023.

"Poet at Work" was originally published in *Voces Cosmicas Signature Series I*. San Antonio Public Library. 2015.

A shorter version of "Catching Ashes" appears in *Weaving the Terrain: 100-Word Southwestern Poems*. Dos Gatos Press. 2017.

"Decomposition" was first published in *riverSedge Issue 36*. University of Texas Rio Grande Valley. 2023.

"Viejito with a Cane" first appeared in *Poetry on the Move*. VIA Metropolitan Transit. 2018.

"Career Choices" was originally published as "The Most Well-Educated Toll Collector" in *riverSedge Issue 34*. University of Texas Rio Grande Valley. 2021.

About the Author

Eddie Vega is a poet, spoken word artist, storyteller, and educator. His poetry has been displayed on VIA Buses, downtown San Antonio buildings, a public park, and the San Pedro Creek Cultural Park. His first full-length collection of poetry, *Chicharra Chorus* (FlowerSong Press) was published in 2019 and he is the 2021 recipient of the Literary Arts Grant from the Luminaria Artist Foundation. In 2022, Vega won the Haiku Death Match at both the Southern Fried Poetry Slam and the NSFPS BlackBerry Peach Slam and was named best local poet by the San Antonio Current. Recently, he edited the collection, *Asina is How We Talk*, poems written by South Texas poets.

Vega writes about food, Tejano culture, social justice, and the intersections thereof. Known as the Taco-Poet of Texas, he is the director and host of The Mouth Dakota Poetry Project, a biweekly open mic in San Antonio, TX.

FLOWERSONG
PRESS

**FlowerSong Press nurtures essential verse
from, about, and throughout the borderlands.
Literary. Lyrical. Boundless.**

Sign up for announcements about
new and upcoming titles at:

www.flowersongpress.com